TECHNIQUES OF ARTIFICIAL INSEMINATION IN CATTLE

by

CAROLYN KEANE

B. S., Kansas State University, 1960

A MASTER'S REPORT

submitted in partial fulfillment of the

requirements for the degree

MASTER OF SCIENCE

Department of Zoology

KANSAS STATE UNIVERSITY
Manhattan, Kansas

1963

Approved by:

Major Professor

TABLE OF CONTENTS

INTRODUCTION

Improvement in livestock has been on the upgrade with the increasing interest and use of artificial insemination (4). In the present day artificial insemination is used on swine, horses, rabbits, dogs, poultry, fur animals, and most extensively used in dairy cattle breeding.

HISTORY OF ARTIFICIAL BREEDING

Thirteen hundred A.D. marks the earliest recording of the employment of artificial insemination (4), (16), (22). Arab horse breeders were known to have collected semen from the better stallions belonging to rival tribes in order to use this semen for the artificial insemination of their mares.

Chronologically in 1780 (1), (18), (21), Spallanzani, an Italian physiologist, conducted the first scientific research concerning the artificial insemination of domestic animals. During this year he successfully inseminated a bitch.

In Europe in 1890, artificial insemination was first used in horse breeding. Professor Hoffman (16), (18) of Stuttgart believed that artificial insemination should follow natural breeding. Once the stallion had served the mare, Hoffman used a speculum and spoon to recover the semen deposited in a depression in the lower vaginal wall. The raw semen was drawn up with a special syringe, diluted with cow's milk, and introduced into the uterus.

In 1902 at the Northern Livestock Conference in Copenhagen, Sand (18) of Denmark noted the important feature of artificial insemination to be the economical use of the semen of a valuable stallion. Sand envisioned the improvement of farm animals through use of this technique.

Twelve years later, Amantea, professor of human physiology at the

University of Rome, was reputed to have devised the first artificial vagina for collection of semen from the dog (5), (18).

However, Russia led by Ivanoff (1), (12), (18) was the first country to use artificial insemination on a large scàle to bring Sand's vision into the realm of reality. Ivanoff started with horses and later succeeded with birds. Moreover, Ivanoff was the first to succeed with cattle and sheep. In 1938 Russia boasted that 120,000 mares, 1,200,000 cattle, and 15,000,000 sheep had been artificially inseminated.

As Ivanoff worked in Russia on the perfection of the artificial insemination technique on a variety of animals, Arthur Walton of England, a pioneer in the field, working with Prawochenski of Poland, experimented with another branch of the technique--the long distance shipping of semen (18). In 1936 sperm were collected from a Suffolk ram at Cambridge, cooled to 10°C, transferred to a thermos flask containing chipped ice, and airmailed to Pulawy Zootechnical Institute in Poland. Five ewes were inseminated with this semen of two to three days old. Two ewes became pregnant. One gave birth to a ram lamb that plainly possessed the Suffolk characteristics.

Also in 1936, the Danes having acquired the technique from the Russians (1), (18), organized a cooperative artificial breeding association. By 1951 approximately fifty-five percent of the nation's dairy cattle had been artificially inseminated.

Enos Perry (1), (18) is credited with establishing the first cooperative dairy cattle artificial breeding association in the United States in May, 1938. By 1954 five million dairy cattle were in artificial insemination programs.

Currently artificial insemination is used mainly in the insemination of cattle and horses (23).

REPRODUCTIVE TRACT OF THE COW

Anatomy

The female reproductive tract provides the ovum, facilitates growth and nourishment of the developing fetus, and later by parturition expels the fully developed fetus (10).

Ovaries. The ovaries, left and right, are 1 1/2 x 1 x 1/2 inches in size and are responsible for periodically producing the ova (1), (7). The size and form varies according to the age and functional activity of the ovary (15). A cross-section of the ovary reveals a Graafian follicle within which the developing ovum is enclosed (1). This follicle matures rapidly from a tiny follicle, for in a period of a week or so it becomes a round, fluid-filled sphere about one-half inch in diameter. At this stage the cow displays heat symptoms.

After heat the Graafian follicle ruptures and the ovum is released. A "meaty" sturcture known as the yellow body or corpus luteum grows in the area where the Graafian follicle collapsed. This body may approach an inch in diameter before beginning a rapid decrease in size (1) just before the next heat 18-24 days later (22). This decrease in size occurs when the ovum remains unfertilized; however, if the ovum is fertilized, the corpus luteum continues its growth until it is quite large (1) and its products apparently suppress heat for the duration of pregnancy (13).

Generally, one follicle followed by one yellow body is formed in one ovary during each estrus (1).

After ovulation, the ovum begins to travel the oviduct. If the ovum is fertilized while in the oviduct, it will follow the oviduct to the uterine horn. If unfertilized, the ovum degenerates and is absorbed while in the oviduct (2).

Oviducts. The oviducts, right and left, also referred to as Fallopian tubes, serve as a route between the vicinity of the ovary and the uterine horn (1), (18). Sperm course the oviduct toward the ovary for fertilization.

The oviduct begins as a thin-walled funnel shaped pouch, partially surrounding the ovary. Then it narrows to a coiled tube an eighteenth to a sixteenth of an inch in diameter which eventually joins the tip of the uterine horn.

Uterus. The uterus is made up of two horns, a right and a left, and a short single body resulting from the connection of the two horns (1), (14), (18). Depending on whether it is a heifer or a cow, a non-pregnant uterus has horns varying in length from 8-10 to 10-15 inches and from 5/8-1 to 1 1/2-2 inches in diameter.

Before joining the cervix, the uterine horns are externally connected for approximately four inches and internally connected for approximately 1 1/2 inches thus forming the body of the uterus.

The wall of a non-pregnant uterus is quite soft and spongy. The lining bears about one hundred small caruncles. These combined with the cotyledons from the fetal membrane, form the "buttons" through which a developing calf is nourished. The fetal membranes, called the afterbirth, must separate from the uterus after calving.

Cervix. The uterus joins the cervix, a single tube-like structure from 2-4 1/2 inches in length and from 3/4 to 2 inches in diameter depending on whether the animal is a cow or a heifer (1).

The cervix is the most important organ of the cow as far as insemination is concerned as it is the target.

This organ is firm and dense to the touch. The forward end blends with the body of the uterus while the backward end is a dome-shaped mass protruding into the vagina and in its approximate center is a depression leading into a canal. The canal through the cervix is lined by a tough membrane of many folds.

In the non-pregnant cow mucus within the cervix is dry and scanty, but becomes more liquid and increases in quantity at the time of heat. During pregnancy, the cervical mucus thickens to a gummy mass called the "cervical seal," which effectively plugs the cervical canal and often covers the opening to the cervix. After the second or thirdmonth of pregnancy, a veterinarian can easily detect the region of the cervix by rectal palpation of this thick mucus.

Vagina. The cervix is joined to the vagina which is 10-12 inches in length, or longer in pregnant or older cows (1), (13). It can be easily distended but is ordinarily collapsed. It is lined by a tough membrane, the folds of which run in the same direction as the passageway. The membranes are well lubricated by mucus especially at the time of heat.

Vulva. The vulva is comprised of two externally located lips and a passage which connects it to the vagina (1). Just within the vulva is the sexually sensitive clitoris and forward a few inches from the clitoris is the opening of the urethra for the passage of urine from the bladder.

Thus, the organ composition of the cow's genital tract, working outwardly is: the ovaries, oviducts, uterine horns, uterine body, cervix, vagina, and vulva.

Physiology

Heat is defined as a short period of female sexual activity signaling the presence of a maturing egg within the ovary (1). During heat the female is under the influence of a sudden high level of the hormone estrogen, produced by the egg-containing follicle.

Heat periods vary in length between six and twenty-seven hours, averaging sixteen hours in the heifer and twenty hours in the cow (22). About seventy per cent show the first signs of heat in the forenoon; others in the afternoon.

At this time the female becomes sexually receptive (1). Detection of heat depends on various signs. The cow shows (a) willingness to stand for mounting by other cows and often herself attempts to ride other cows. Ruffed hair over the tail head suggests that a cow has recently been ridden. (Cows sniffing each other is a common sign that one is approaching or is in early heat). The cow also shows (b) willingness to stand for and accept the service of the bull; (c) some swelling of the vulva, the lips of which become moist and less wrinkled; and (d) the discharge of thin, clear, highly lubricant mucus often in strands from the vulva. The mucus is smeared on the buttocks, over the pin bones and under the tail. Finally, the cow displays nervousness, a tendency to bawl, a decrease in appetite, and usually a decrease in milk production.

The egg is shed after the close of heat (1). Professor S. A. Asdell

sperm accumulate within the epididymis (1). The vas deferens carries the sperm from the epididymis to the urethra. The urethra is the canal through the penis providing common passage from the body for either urine or semen.

The seminal vesicles, evaginations of the ampulla which is the dilated posterior region of the vas deferens (2); prostate gland; and the bulbourethral glands are found near the area where the sperm and urine enter the urethra (1). A short distance from these above mentioned accessory glands is a third pair called the Cowper's glands (23). The accessory glands in combination produce the fluid environment for the sperm. This fluid plus the sperm constitutes semen. The fluids help transport the sperm, supply the proper environment to keep the sperm alive, and clean the urethra prior to the time of ejaculation. It is also thought that the alkaline secretion of the prostate gland is of apparent value in neutralizing any acidic condition of the urethra and also the vagina (10).

Penis. The penis is the means by which semen is deposited in the vagina during natural breeding (1). As sexual excitement mounts, blood accumulates within the penis, thereby causing an increase in diameter and length and a decrease in structural flexibility. This additional length during erection is attributed to the obliteration of a "S" shaped curve, the sigmoid flexure, in the penis located at the level of the scrotum. At the peak of excitement the bull makes a deep single thrust of the penis into the cow's vagina or artificial vagina and ejaculation occurs.

The volume of the ejaculate varies with age, breed, and frequency of service as does the concentration of the sperm and the percentage of them that are vigorous.

The normal ejaculation is somewhere between four and ten cubic

centimeters and if of good quality, it contains 1500 million sperm, a
ratio of 100 million per drop, of which 60-80 per cent should be vigorous
and actually motile.

COLLECTION SCHEDULE

The collection of semen is set up on a schedule adapted to the individual bull (19). Some of the average bulls produce their best semen if
it is collected on a weekly basis, whereas bulls producing large quantities
of heavy semen often perform best on a four to five day schedule. Young
bulls are often collected from on a ten day schedule. Collecting too often
lowers semen quality and concentration.

Bulls that have been running with females in the breeding pasture
should be kept away seven to ten days before collecting their semen for
freezing purposes.

Bulls which have neither been subjected to collection nor exposed to
females in heat for several months should have a series of weekly collections
before setting the date for collections and freezing.

More satisfactory results are noted when a bull has been confined and
an accurate observation has been made on his semen quality and production.

Methods of Collection

There are four possible methods of semen collection: (a) from the
vagina of the cow; (b) by massage of the bull's ampullae; (c) by electro-
ejaculation; and (d) by use of an artificial vagina (1), (18), (19). Of
the four methods the artificial vagina and the electro-ejaculator are
satisfactory for use in an artificial insemination program.

Vaginal Collection. This is the simplest method of collection whereby
the semen is collected from the floor of the vagina following copulation (4).
Collection is accomplished by use of either a long handled vaginal spoon or
a syringe and nozzle.

This method is seldom used today as semen collected in this manner is
badly contaminated with secretions of the female and there is great danger
of spreading disease (23).

Massage. This method is recommended only in case of valuable bulls
that are lame, or for some other reason will not mount (18).

The bull is tied in a stall or restrained in a squeeze chute, in a
manner in which he cannot shift from side to side (4). By a few stroking
movements, the sheath of the penis is rid of any residual urine in order to
prevent urine contamination (17), (18). The end hairs of the sheath are
now clipped. The sheath is washed with warm water by using a soft brush to
partly induce urination as urine is toxic to sperm.

This technique requires the assistance of two operators. One operator
holds a collecting funnel under the end of the penis at the prepuce while
the other does the actual massage of the ampullae (4), (18). The operator
doing the massaging must have short fingernails and must wear a long-
sleeved rubber glove as arm protection.

The glove and anus of the bull are well-lubricated before the operator
inserts his arm into the rectum. Once inside the rectum, the operator re-
moves the feces. The gloved hand is then inserted seven to ten inches into
the rectum and the seminal vesicles are massaged by backward strokes and
their contents, seminal fluid containing relatively few sperm, is thus expelled (4). The operator now locates the ampullae by protruding his hand

forward enough so that his fingers fall over the anterior edge of the pelvic
bone. Then by drawing his arm backwards and by applying a gentle downward
pressure of the hand, his fingers fall into a triangular space formed by
the two ampullae. The ampullae are massaged by the "stripping technique"
where the second finger of the hand is run between the two ampullae while
the thumb and third finger are placed on the outer sides of the ampullae (18).
A slow rhythmic motion must be practiced with this method. The fluid from
the ampullae is rich in spermatozoa (4).

Electro-ejaculation. The electro-ejaculator was developed in 1950
for use in collecting semen from physically disabled bulls and from those
who failed to serve the artificial vagina (19).

The bull is restrained in a squeeze chute so as to restrict side to
side movement. In addition, an adjustable pole is placed behind the rear
legs in order to reduce extension as much as possible. As a third precaution,
a sling or rope arrangement should be placed behind the front legs so that
the bull cannot go completely down as many often do just before ejaculation.
Since sunlight is harmful to semen, the squeeze chute desirably should be
placed in a sheltered area.

Electrodes, to which the electrical current is controlled, are inserted
into the rectum of the bull after the feces have been removed with a salt
solution. The electrodes are held so that the current passing through them
stimulates nerves at the root of the penis near the accessory glands. A
few stimulations of low voltage serve to cause a slight erection and a
passage of semen which can be collected by means of a funnel and tube (4).

Marder (9) developed a lucite probe, 13 inches long and 1 7/8 inches
in diameter, inlaid lengthwise with four brass electrodes for use in this

technique. A device to reduce voltage and control current completed the apparatus. To begin with the rectum is flushed of its contents. The probe is then placed in a pail of warm water, removed and inserted into the rectum of the bull far enough so that only the cable remains outside. The probe is placed centrally on the floor of the rectum.

The stimulus is applied by gradually increasing the intensity of the current into the electrodes for about five seconds and then returning to zero for ten seconds allowing a rest period before further stimulation. This pattern of stimulation and rest is continued until ejaculation which usually occurs within three minutes.

During stimulation there is a gradual rise to the maximum voltage of 5.5 accompanied by a gradual increase in current up to 900 ma. Ideally erection and ejaculation occur. The semen is collected in a rubber funnel attached to a test tube surrounded by a water bath maintained at approximately $90^{\circ}F$ (19).

This method is best performed by two men. One man operates the electro-ejaculator and keeps the rectal probe in position while the second man collects the sperm. If the protrusion of the penis is affected the collector can use one hand to hold the penis steady while using the other to hold the collecting apparatus. Care should be taken on the collector's part only to catch the sperm-rich fraction of the ejaculate as post-ejaculatory fluids have a detrimental effect on the motility of the sperm cells and a very small amount of this fluid can render the entire collection useless.

Managers of breeding organizations report that semen collected by this method is seldom of the quality of that collected by the artificial vagina (17), (18). However, satisfactory fertility rates have followed its use (9).

Artificial Vagina. The artificial vagina is the preferred method of
collection if the bull is capable of mounting the tease animal (19). This
without a doubt is the quickest and easiest method whereby a complete physiological collection can be obtained more often than using an electro-
ejaculator. The major disadvantage is the possible injury to the bull
during mounting of the tease animal. Injury rarely occurs if footing is
adequate and the tease animal is properly restrained.

The artificial vagina consists of a heavy rubber or canvas outer
jacket; a rubber cylinder, 14-16 inches long and about two and three-fourths
inches in diameter; a latex inner lining drawn through and folded back over
each end of the cylinder; and a latex cone to which a graduated collecting
tube is attached (9). The artificial vagina is held together by strong
rubber bands around each end. Care should be taken in placing the rubber
band on the open end because of the danger that it might slip off and en-
circle the penis during the thrust. It is safer to fix the inner lining
to the cylinder by a piece of heavy cord.

The collecting tube is often held against the side of the vagina by
means of a small rubber band in order to keep the tube warm. An insulated
jacket may be placed over the cylinder in order to protect the collecting
tube from the sunlight and reduce heat loss from the cylinder (19).

The artificial vagina is now filled with water heated to $125^{o}F$ and
permitted to stand until the internal temperature reaches 110°-$115^{o}F$.
Pressure within is controlled by the amount of water. The pressure should
be adequate to cause the reflex stimulus resulting in ejaculation. Excess
pressure may cause inflammation of the penis and in this case semen is deposited high in the artificial vagina and will not flow freely to the

collecting tube resulting in damage of the semen by the higher temperature in the upper region of the artificial vagina. Moreover, if the pressure is too great, the collecting tube may be forced out when the bull thrusts.

The opening of the inner lining is evenly and thoroughly smeared with a thin coat of lubricant, non-toxic to sperm (4). The lubricant is limited to the first six inches of the lining and this aids in preventing bacterial contamination from the penis.

Now the artificial vagina is ready for use. The bull is led behind the tease animal and the collector follows on the bull's right side, grasping the artificial vagina in the right hand, pointing the mouth downward (4). Care should be taken by the collector to brace his shoulder against the bull (19). This gives the bull a sense of security and also if the bull falls the collector will be pushed away (14), (19).

When the bull mounts, the apparatus is inserted behind and to the outside of the bull's foreleg with the opening directed toward the penis at a 45° angle (4), (14), (19). The collector directs the penis into the opening of the artificial vagina by applying the left hand to the sheath. Force should not be applied when guiding the penis into the artificial vagina as this may cause the bull to retract the penis (19). When the penis comes in contact with the warm, lubricated surface of the artificial vagina, the bull thrusts upward and ejaculates (4), (19). The collector must be careful not to touch the penis or the bull may retract it and dismount.

The semen is ejaculated into the upper end of the graduated collecting tube. Immediately the apparatus should be turned downward to allow the semen to flow into the tube.

The success of the collection depends on the conditioning of the bull, psychologically and sexually (18). This conditioning concerns associating the bull with the tease animal and servicing of the artificial vagina by the bull. For most bulls, the steer is the first choice of tease animal (19) once the bull is accustomed to the process. A steer will stand better for the bull and is easy to handle. Using a cow, especially one in heat, presents the danger of the bull serving the cow if the collector is negligent. Also if the cow is in heat, the bull often becomes excessively excited and hard to handle. Semen from an over-stimulated bull varies in concentration and quality.

Once the bull becomes adjusted to the tease cow or steer and associates the collection quarters to sexual excitement, a dummy cow may be substituted for the teaser (18), (19). The dummy must be strongly constructed, preferably a metal framework adequate to support the weight of the largest bull. The dummy cow should bear some resemblance to a female, should be well padded on the top and sides, and covered with a hide or canvas. The artificial vagina can be held in place by a spring-like attachment, by straps, or by someone seated under the dummy.

Any bull capable of mounting can be collected from by means of the artificial vagina (19). While it may take considerable time and work to get the bull to serve the first time, once he has served collection becomes easier. Bulls requiring the most stimulation are restrained so they can watch a bull from which semen is being collected. These bulls should then be allowed one or two false mounts in order to stimulate them to have an erection before mounting the tease animal for actual collection purposes. Twice or more than twice as many sperm per ejaculate can be obtained by subjecting the bull to the teasing mentioned above.

When collection has been accomplished, the vial of semen is set in the laboratory pending examination. Meanwhile, the artificial vagina is thoroughly cleansed (4). First it is taken apart and each section washed in soap and water, rinsed in distilled water, followed by boiling or rinsing in ethyl alcohol. If the artificial vagina is to be used within twenty-four hours after rinsing in alcohol, it must be rinsed in physiological saline as alcohol is harmful to spermatozoa.

SEMEN EXAMINATION

The vial of semen is labeled as soon as it is collected with the name and number of the bull, the breed, the date, and the volume of the semen (11).

Semen Characteristics

Normally semen has a color that approximates that of whole milk. A yellow color may indicate admixture of urine, or it may be normal. If there is a pinkish cast to the semen, this indicates the presence of blood. While the ejaculate may be normally fertile, the source of the blood should be determined (19).

The volume of the ejaculate (18) usually is proportional to the body weight of the animal. Yearlings may yield only a few cubic centimeters; whereas, older bulls may yield between six and twelve cubic centimeters. Healthy bulls of both dairy and beef breeds average 5-6 cc. A mature sire may yield 1-15 cc.

The difference in volume may be due to the intensity of sexual preparation, before collection, that is the time of restraint before mounting or the number of false mounts.

Semen is composed of two portions, seminal plasma and spermatozoa
(15). The former are secretions of the accessory sexual glands. Normally
little more than one-half the ejaculate is made up of these secretions which
function to facilitate the ejaculation of the concentrated sperm fraction
(18). Healthy seminal plasma is almost constant in characteristics (14).
Variations in appearance are mainly relative to the number of spermatozoa
concentrated in it.

Bull sperm appear much like miniature tadpoles as they swim, lashing
their tails (23). Usually there are 300 million to two billion per cubic
centimeter in bull semen. While volume is important, sperm number is more
important (14).

Microscopic Examination

Motility. Examination of sperm for motility, although it has its
limitations, is the most useful criterion for evaluating semen quality (4).
The method of collection greatly affects motility. Vaginal samples are
rarely used as the life of the sperm is short-lived in the vagina. The
most reliable results are obtained from samples collected in the artificial
vagina.

Motility evaluation is based on (a) the per cent motility which in
turn is the visual estimate of the number of actively moving sperm in a
semen sample, in terms of the total sperm present, in increments of 10%;
and (b) the rate of motility, based on the type and speed of the forward
movement of the sperm (18). The four types of bull sperm motility generally
seen are (a) progressive; (b) a circular movement confined to a radius ap-
proximating the length of the sperm; (c) vibratory side-to-side motion in a

static position associated with aged semen; and (d) reverse-sperm in back-ward motion.

According to Herman (10), preparation for motility examination follows these logical steps:

1. Warm a clean glass slide to approximately 100°F.

2. Mix the semen by inverting the vial two or three times.

3. Place one drop of semen on the warmed slide and spread the drop. A coverslip may be used to aid in spreading.

4. Examine for motility with the low power objective. A microscope with a regulated stage incubator is desirable to rewarm the slide, if necessary, during examination (18).

5. Observe the semen around the edges of the coverslip to ascertain the approximation of the per cent of live, active sperm.

6. Observe the overall movement in the drop.

7. Classify the motility.

The state of Missouri recommends this classification rating:

5 - excellent motility. Eighty per cent or more of the spermatozoa are in very vigorous motion. Swirls and eddies formed by the movements of the sperm are extremely rapid and changing constantly.

4 - very good motility. Approximately 70-80% of the sperm are in vigorous motion. Swirls and eddies form and drop rapidly but not as rapidly as a 5 rating.

3 - good motility. About 50-75% of the sperm are in motion. The motion is vigorous, but the waves and eddies formed move slowly across the field.

2 - fair motility. Twenty to fifty per cent of the sperm are in motion.

Movements are largely vigorous, but no waves or eddies are formed.

1 - poor motility. Less than 30% of the sperm are in motion. The motion is weak and oscillatory and not progressive.

0 - no motion visible.

Experience soon enables an examiner to estimate the percentage of viable sperm causing the swirling motions (4).

Methylene Blue Reduction. Whereas visual examination of semen to determine per cent motility is adequate, many technicians prefer to augment this exam with the methylene blue reduction test which serves as an indi- cation of the number and activity of the sperm (10), (14).

Oxygen is used at a more rapid rate in semen containing a high con- centration of active sperm than in poor quality semen (10). This causes an excess of hydrogen which combines with the methylene blue to form leucomethylene blue. The relative length of time this bleaching out or reduction of the blue color requires indicates the number and activity of the sperm.

Preparation for the test involves the following steps:

1. Prepare the methylene blue solution by dissolving 50 mg. of methylene blue in 100 ml. of 3.6% sodium citrate buffer.
2. Dilute the semen (.2 ml.) with .8 ml. egg-yolk citrate diluter in a 10 ml. vial and mix thoroughly.
3. Add .1 ml. of methylene blue and mix.
4. Seal the tube with one-half inch layer of mineral oil.
5. Place in a hot water bath between 110° and 115° F.
6. Observe the time required for the sample to lose its color.

If the blue color is lost in 3-6 minutes, the quality of the semen is good. Any sample containing color after nine minutes should not be used for insemination because in such a sample few sperm are alive or all are dead.

VanDenmark (4) and his co-workers found high and significant correlations between this reduction time and the volume of ejaculate, sperm count, initial sperm motility, and initial pH.

Sperm Count. The number of spermatozoa per unit volume is an important consideration in determining the optimum dilution ratio for artificial insemination work (10). Also the sperm count is helpful in determining the fertility of the bull. Fertility is determined not only by the number of sperm, but by the per cent of live sperm and the degree of motility.

There are various methods of counting sperm:

1. Hemocytometer method:

    (a) Mix the semen well by inverting the vial three times.

    (b) Draw .05 ml. of semen into the standard red cell dilution pipette to the mark below the bulb.

    (c) Draw a small bubble of air into the pipette and wipe the end of the pipette clean. The air bubble prevents capillary removal of semen during the cleaning before dipping into the diluting fluid.

    (d) Fill the pipette to the 1.01 mark with a diluting fluid, usually 3% NaCl.

    (e) Agitate the pipette for three minutes to insure mixing.

    (f) Discard the first four to five drops.

    (g) Place a cover glass over the ruled field of a cytometer and let the drop run under the cover glass.

(h) Make the count under low magnification. When using the
improved Neubauer ruled counting chamber, it is best to
count the 5 large double ruled squares over the field.
This will give a total count of 80 small squares. The
number of sperm counted times 10,000 equals the sperm
concentration per cubic centimeter of semen.

If diluted semen is used this figure must be multiplied by the
dilution ratio to determine the sperm concentration. For counting purposes
dilution fluid may consist of 50 cc. of distilled water, two cubic centimeters of 2% eosin to provide background and facilitate counting, and one
cubic decimeter of 3% NaCl solution to kill the sperm and prevent movement.

2. Photoelectric colorimeter:

For present day breeding organizations the photoelectric colorimeter is the best and most practical means of making sperm counts so
that each bull's semen can be so diluted as to insure enough sperm
for every insemination (18). The instrument must be standardized
against known sperm concentrations as determined by the hemocytometer
method before using routinely.

This method is based on the amount of light passing through a standard
dilution of semen, usually one part semen to ten parts of M/15 sodium citrate
(10). Once the optical density is read from the colorimeter, it is compared
to a chart which has been carefully constructed to estimate sperm count at
the varying optical density percentages.

While this may be a practical means of counting sperms, the method is
not widely used as the equipment and technical experience are not generally
available.

Dead-Alive Staining. The hemocytometer and colorimeter methods determine the number of sperm present; however, information regarding how many
of these sperm are dead or alive is necessary when dealing with semen to be
frozen for future use. The dead-alive staining technique (10) is based on
the difference between live and dead sperm in absorbing certain dyes. Sperm
that are dead at the time of staining will absorb the stain while sperm that
are alive will not; therefore, they remain clear while the dead ones appear
blue.

A stain commonly used consists of one per cent eosin and four per cent
aniline blue dissolved in M/8 phosphate buffer. One to two drops of stain
are placed on a clean glass slide and mixed with a small amount of semen.
A second slide is placed over the first, the excess stain is removed with a
cloth; and then the slides are drawn apart quickly and dried by placing on
a hot plate at 150-200°F. The slide is mounted on the microscope and counted
under the high dry objective (430X) or the oil immersion objective (970X).
Generally a total of 333 sperm are counted and per cent alive computed:

$$\frac{\text{Number of live sperm counted X 3}}{10} = \text{\% alive sperm}$$

Dr. James Forgason of Winrock Farm, Morrilton, Arkansas, counts 100
sperm under the oil immersion lens. The count is registered on a counting
machine which is manually operated. This machine has a series of keys two
of which are used in counting sperm. One key is used to tally the number of
live sperm viewed while the other tallies the number of dead sperm viewed.
A bell rings when the count reaches 100 and the per cent alive can be read
directly from the counter.

Semen Morphology. An excessive number of abnormal sperm will lower the probable fertility of the semen. Thus an additional test must be run in determining the value of a particular sample of semen for future artificial insémination (10). High quality semen should not contain more than 5-15% abnormal sperm; average semen contains 10-20% abnormalities while poor quality may contain as high as 30% abnormalities.

Before venturing into the causes of abnormalities, the term "abnormalities" bears explanation (2). The normal sperm consists of an oval-shaped head connected posteriorly to a short neck followed by the body of the sperm. The body is a "connecting piece" belonging to the tail and it is slightly longer than the head. The body consists of a central core known as the axial filament which is beset with mitochondrial granules and it is bounded anteriorly and posteriorly by centrioles. The third and last part of the sperm is the tail. The tail tapers to a point. The anterior part is a continuation of the cytoplasmic sheathed axial filament of the neck and the posterior part is the axial filament minus the sheath.

Abnormalities in sperm may occur in one, two, or in all three main sections. Bent tails have been found to be the most common abnormality (4). Perhaps the sperm may have coiled tails, may be tailless, may have a pyriform head, a tapering head, a small head, a double head and body, a double tail, an undeveloped body, or an abnormal body (11).

The presence of a large number of abnormalities may be indicative of spermatic derangement or abnormality of the reproductive tract with consequent reduction in fertility (4). Blom discovered that primary abnormalities in bull semen were due to disorders in the spermatic epithelium. He found a 4.65 to 10.4 percentage of primary abnormalities in the semen from 100 normal fertile bulls. If this percentage rose over 15%, the fertility of the bull

was impaired and in many cases testis degeneration or testis hypoplasia
was noted.

Secondary abnormalities appear as the result of some adverse condition
after the semen has passed from the spermatic epithelium. Sperm of males
that do not copulate frequently collect in the afferent ducts where they
eventually undergo degeneration. If such a situation occurs these bulls
should have two ejaculates collected at one session. If the abnormalities
continue to appear, testis degeneration may have begun.

The following procedure for determining the percentage abnormality
is outlined by Herman (10).

1. Place 2-3 drops of any physiological buffer on a clean slide.

2. Add one drop of mixed semen.

3. Spread by covering with a second slide.

4. Air dry the smear thoroughly.

5. Stain with Rose Bengal Stain.

6. Dry and count.

Generally a total of 333 sperm are counted using random fields. The count
is done under the high dry objective. The total of abnormal sperm counted
is then multiplied by three and divided by ten to give the percentage of
abnormalities.

SEMEN DILUTION

The next step in semen processing is dilution of the sample for freezing
purposes. Therefore, the evaluation processes must be done carefully as a
failure of the semen during one of these steps is nearly always indicative
of a failure in freezing the semen (19).

After collection of the semen, as has been mentioned before, a visual examination concerning appearance as rated with normal and a sperm count are performed. If the semen, at this stage, displays the qualities needed in artificial insemination, the remainder of the collection is poured into a test tube containing 10 cc. of egg-yolk citrate diluter. If the raw semen remains undiluted during the entirety of the evaluation processes, the sperm cells rapidly deteriorate as the metabolites are being used up by the active sperm and the by-products of this oxidation are lactic acid and carbon dioxide which have an adverse effect on motility and longevity of the sperm cells. Care must be taken that the 10 cc. of diluter and semen are at the same temperature, preferably room temperature, for if the diluter were cooler the sperm would undergo cold shock and many would be damaged or would perish (18), (19), (23).

Before progressing further on the topic of actual dilution procedure, it is necessary to outline the object of dilution. The primary purpose of dilution is to increase the volume of the ejaculate of the male so that it may be used to inseminate a larger number of females (4). A good diluter (a) must not be toxic to the sperm; (b) must have an osmotic relationship similar to that of undiluted semen; (c) has a pH favorable for continued viability of the sperm; (d) should contain a buffering solution to protect against marked changes in hydrogen-ion concentration; (3) should increase the length of time semen can be stored without loss in fertility; (f) should be inexpensive to prepare and easy to prepare; and (g) should prevent injury from cold shock. A diluter containing added egg yolk, developed by Lardy and Phillips for use in handling bull semen, has served as the nucleus around which other formulas have evolved.

The most common diluter of the day is the egg-yolk sodium citrate mixture (1). Fresh non-fertile eggs from disease free flocks are collected twelve hours after laying. The eggs are broken individually in order to separate the yolk from the white. The yolk is poured back and forth from one half-shell to the other to remove as much yolk from the white as possible. The yolk is then placed on a sterile 2"x2" piece of cardboard with a one-fourth inch hole in the center. The cardboard is resting above a glass beaker. A sterile glass rod is used to punch a hole through the yolk membrane permitting the yolk to drain into the beaker.

The yolk is mixed in a one to four ratio with a 2.4-2.9 per cent sodium citrate dehydrate solution which is prepared with distilled water, then boiled, autoclaved, and cooled (24). After the yolk and citrate are well mixed, 1000 units of penicillin and 1000 micrograms of streptomycin per millimeter of extender are added.

A Colorado State University laboratory has chosen to use the yolk-citrate diluter as it is easier when performing microscopic examinations of the semen to see the sperm as the fat globules in a milk base distender make distinguishing of the individual sperm cells rather difficult (19).

A second part of the extender must now be prepared. However, before proceeding, the final number of ampules to be frozen needs determining (19). This number is arrived at by multiplying the cell count by the percentage alive and multiplying this answer by the volume of raw semen, thus calculating the number of sperm cells alive per collection per bull. The number of live cells from each collection is added to the numbers of the live cells found in other samples by the same bull. This total is divided by thirty million as thirty million is the number of sperm placed in each ampule. Under average conditions 60% of the live, motile cells will recover following freezing; thus, by placing thirty million per ampule the optimum inseminating dosage of ten million live, progressively motile sperm will be present at the time of use (19).

With the number of ampules determined, final dilution may proceed. Samples from the same bull are poured together. One-half of the final volume of diluter is added to the mixture of semen and the original ten cubic centimeters of diluter. This new dilution is mixed gently (10) and placed in a 30°C. waterbath for approximately ten minutes (19). The diluted semen is then transferred to a 5°C. cold room. The time required for the temperature to drop from 30°C. to 5°C. is approximately two hours. The cooling rate should never exceed 1°C/4 minutes. The walk-in cold room is the best for maintaining this rate.

The diluted semen stands in the cold room from four to six hours allowing the antibiotics to work. This step has been taken because it has been shown that glycerol, found in the second part of the diluter, inhibits the effectiveness of the antibiotics (24).

Preparation of this second part requires the addition of fourteen parts glycerol to eighty-six parts of the yolk-citrate solution (19). Glycerol has been found to enhance the fertility of frozen semen. This solution is stored in the cold room. The glycerol-yolk-citrate solution may be added dropwise with constant gentle mixing to the already dilute and cool semen or one-third aliquots may be gently mixed in at ten minute intervals. Agitation must be done carefully as to prevent oxygen from mixing with sperm as it is harmful. Either method should take twenty to thirty minutes. The total volume of yolk-citrate-glycerol solution should equal

the volume of the originally diluted semen. In this way a concentration
of seven per cent glycerol is obtained in the final mixture to be frozen.
The above mixing is done at the maintained five degree Centigrade temperature.

Many workers in the field believe that improved fertility of a frozen
sample results if this final dilution remains in the cold room at least
twelve hours to allow equilibration between the semen and glycerol. Others,
working at Illinois University, suggest little or no time be allotted after
glycerization before actual freezing (24).

After equilibration with the glycerol, the semen is placed in one
millimeter portions in 1.2 ml. or 2 ml. vials or ampules which are then
sealed (19). Loading ampules can be done with an automatic syringe or
pipette provided a large-gaged needle is used. Care must also be taken
not to force the mixture rapidly through the syringe as this is likely to
injure the sperm. The ampule is then sealed automatically.

The ampule is identified by the bull's name, registration number,
and freezing date. Ampules may be pre-marked by the Markem printing
machine and then sterilized in high dry heat which not only frees ampules
of harmful bacteria but also fixes the ink on the glass.

HISTORY OF SEMEN FREEZING

Nineteen hundred and fifty-one marks the announcement of the first
successful impregnation of a cow with bull semen that had been frozen (24).
This achievement stimulated much interest and research in freezing as a
method of preserving bull semen.

However, the discovery that semen can withstand freezing dates back
to 1897 when Davenport found that human sperm were alive after being frozen.

In 1949 Polge and Parkes at the British Institute of Medical Research in Kindon, demonstrated that by adding glycerol to fowl semen it would survive freezing. In 1950 bull semen survived freezing upon the addition of glycerol.

Thus in 1951 frozen semen was used to produce a calf in England and a lamb in Australia.

FREEZING SEMEN

The marked ampules are placed in racks and lowered into a bath of isopropyl alcohol or acetone (11) which has been cooled to $5^{\circ}C$. (24).

The bath may be in a wide mouth thermos or an insulated container of almost any sort having a large opening at the top. The size of the container varies directly with the number of ampules to be frozen.

The alcohol or acetone bath and the ampules of semen are cooled by adding chipped or ground dry ice (24) or liquid carbon dioxide (8) at a controlled rate. The accepted rate of freezing is $1-2^{\circ}C$. per minute (11), (24) from $5^{\circ}C$. to minus $20^{\circ}C$. and a rate of $3-4^{\circ}C$. from minus $20^{\circ}C$. to minus $79^{\circ}C$. The freezing rate is the critical factor in determining the percentage of sperm that will survive the process (19).

For optimum freezing it is essential to have definite control of this freezing rate. Electrical machines (24), a mechanical agitator, a dial thermometer ranging from minus $100^{\circ}C$. to plus $40^{\circ}C$. and a clock (11) are commercially available to regulate the rate of cooling and facilitate the freezing procedure (11), (24).

Storage. Once the freezing has been completed, the ampules are ready for moving from the alcohol bath to the storage area. The type of storage depends on the availability of dry ice or liquid nitrogen in an area (19). This availability plus the cost of the storage container, the operating expense and the volume of semen are determining factors in individual circumstances.

Dry ice and alcohol maintain the maximum low storage temperature of minus 79°C. or minus 110°F. (24). After freezing the semen is placed in well-insulated containers of styrofoam covered with a metal outer-covering and thermos inner-covering (19). The containers are kept supplied with dry ice and alcohol (9). This method of storage is simple and relatively cheap, and the containers come in various sizes and can thus fit many sized operations in the field (11). A disadvantage is that a constant supply of dry ice must be available to keep the storage equipment properly supplied.

If the semen is to be stored in liquid nitrogen, then the semen is transferred to nitrogen storage tanks from the alcohol bath (8). Liquid nitrogen is the fourth coldest substance known (11). At atmospheric pressure, the boiling point is minus 196°C. or minus 320°F. Growing evidence suggests that temperatures below minus 79°C. may be more desirable for semen storage. The nitrogen storage tanks require the addition of refrigerant every two to three weeks (19). The disadvantage to this method is the high cost of liquid nitrogen.

The above two methods of storage require transferring of the ampules from the alcohol or acetone bath to the storage tanks. Dr. J. L. Forgason, veterinarian for Winrock Farm, Morrilton, Arkansas; W. T. Berry, Jr., Operations Manager of Winrock; and Dr. D. E. Goodwin, veterinarian for Kermas Angus Ranch have developed a method of directly freezing the semen in the

liquid nitrogen vapor refrigeration units thus eliminating the need for
transferring.

These three men froze semen from two Santa Gortrudus bulls, a total of
372 ampules, by two methods: (a) the carbon dioxide and alcohol bath and
(b) in nitrogen vapor. The rate of freezing in the alcohol bath was regulated by a cam controlled electrical valve maintaining a temperature drop
from $5^{o}C$. to minus $15^{o}C$. at a rate of $3^{o}C$. per minute and from minus $15^{o}C$.
to minus $50^{o}C$. at a rate of $5^{o}C$. per minute.

There was no control on the freezing rate of the semen in the liquid
nitrogen vapor. The ampules were placed directly in the liquid nitrogen
refrigeration units and the freezing rate was determined by a thermocouple
which registered the rate to be $2.5^{o}C$. per minute from $5^{o}C$. to minus $15^{o}C$.
and $6^{o}C$. per minute from minus $15^{o}C$. to minus $50^{o}C$. The average survival
rate of the sperm was 65.7% compared to 68.3% in the carbon dioxide-alcohol
bath. The latter result is not statistically different from that of the
liquid nitrogen.

KABSU (Kansas Artificial Breeding Service Unit at Manhattan, Kansas)
is presently using this method in freezing many of their semen ampules (6).
They have a new freezer in operation which acts as a vaporizing mechanism
transferring first vapor and then liquid nitrogen into a refrigerator can
containing unfrozen semen. This service lists the following reasons for
using liquid nitrogen for both freezing and storage. Liquid nitrogen (a)
makes up 4/5's of the air by volume; (b) does not combine or react with
other elements; (c) in a free state will not support combustion or burn;
(d) is colorless and odorless, but must be handled with care as it will
injure the skin similar to a burn; (e) is the most economical refrigerant

for the low temperature maintained; and (f) holds a temperature between 320°F. to 265°F. below zero.

Frozen Semen Evaluation. Careful timely checks need to be made on frozen semen to determine the percentage of sperm that continue living under subzero conditions (19). While microscopic checks reveal the percentage alive, the importance of a freeze is not exhibited until the cow is inseminated.

Colorado follows these steps in evaluating frozen semen:

1. Wash a slide in distilled water, dry thoroughly, and place in a 100°F. warmer.

2. Thaw sample ampules of semen in ice water, allowing ten minutes for thawing.

3. With an eye dropper place one drop of semen on the warmed slide.

4. Place a coverslip over the drop.

5. Allow five minutes and then examine under the high powered objective.

6. Estimate the per cent motile and determine the rate of motility as described in previous examinations.

By comparing the percentage alive before and after freezing, the number of motile cells per inseminating dose can be determined. For satisfactory use each ampule must contain at least ten million live sperm cells with a motility grade of three or more.

Advantages and Disadvantages of Frozen Semen. The list of advantages for semen freezing is definitely more impressive than that for the disadvantages, but both sides need be presented for careful evaluation of the process.

Advantage-wise, frozen semen (a) extends the use and more efficient
utilization of semen from proven sires; therefore, obtaining maximum production rates per bull (19); (b) can be transported for selective matings
nearly anywhere in the world; (c) carries on the influence of valuable
bulls long after they are gone (18); (d) is valuable in the artificial
insemination of beef cattle as semen can be processed and stored before
the breeding season to insure possible breeding of a large number of females
to a single bull in a four to six week period (19). Usage of frozen semen
by beef cattle producers is yearly on the upward trend as the breeders want
the very best sires and the commercial producer wants efficient gain (18).
Finally transportation costs of semen from a bull stud to area technicians
is greatly reduced as a supply can be stocked for several weeks. Semen
is shipped in dry ice containers where the ampules are in a plastic bag
containing alcohol and the bag is surrounded by crushed dry ice (19).
Shipping in a small liquid nitrogen container is becoming more popular
for the large scale operations.

The list of disadvantages, while not as long, is valid. Some bulls
(18), about one-third, produce semen that will not undergo the rigors of
freezing. Thus, unless care is taken, bulls may be largely selected on a
"fertility basis," and some of the better production bulls may be ignored
due to the fact they are low in fertility. Fertility is important and should
be stressed; however, in the present day competitive program in artificial
insemination which really demands "get the cow settled" some very great
sires may be lightly used.

In addition frozen semen is expensive. The cost of dry ice or liquid
nitrogen and the maintenance of a semen bank is a daily expense. Yet, frozen

semen seems to be the ideal answer for cattlemen wanting selected matings.

Lastly, heavy utilization of frozen semen limits the number of sires used. There is no argument as to the wisdom of heavily using a bull of greatness to sire many progeny. The question arising is "what sire or sires should be entrusted with a man's herd?" If selection methods were perfect, no argument would exist. One side says not to use too few sires while on the other hand when truly great bulls are found to meet the present day's appraisal, their heavy use can add much to the genetic "bank account" for cattle.

LIQUID SEMEN

Liquid semen is the coming answer to using semen that will not withstand freezing. It is diluted and cooled like semen which is to be frozen, but it is simply stored at 5°C. (8). The reduced temperature slows down the sperm until they are inactive (23) and also keeps bacterial growth at a minimum (18). Sperm will live under this condition for a week or more, but there is a drop in fertility. For this reason, liquid semen is used for only three days after collection (8).

INSEMINATION TECHNIQUES

The semen samples are held at storage temperatures until needed. When a cow to be bred appears in heat, she is moved to the insemination paddocks and an ampule of semen is removed from storage for thawing and eventual insemination. Semen is thawed by placing the ampule in a 5°C. ice water bath (1), (24). Once thawed this semen should be used within a few minutes.

The cow to be inseminated must be normal, free from diseases of the reproductive system, and in good breeding condition (4). She is confined in a stall or stanchion equipped with a good light from behind. The vulva is wiped clean with cotton or washed using warm water, soap, and a disinfectant, rinsed in clear water, and dried by spreading the lips and swabbing with clean cotton.

An attendant holds the tail aside and the cow is now ready for insemination which artifically can be done by one of two methods. The speculum method allows the cervix to be observed during the insemination (9). The point of the inseminating tube is then gently inserted from one to two centimeters into the lumen of the cervix, and semen is slowly expelled into the cervix by gentle pressure on the syringe plunger (4). The semen should stay in the cervix and not flow back. Also care should be taken to make sure the speculum used is of small enough diameter so the cow will not arch her back and strain. This method is seldom employed at the present time as it does not allow deep penetration of the cervix.

The cervical fixation or rectal method (4) has taken precedence to the speculum method. In this technique the technician wears a rubber or disposable (1) plastic glove-sleeve combination on the hand to enter the rectum and a wrist-length glove on the other hand. He approaches the cow quietly, confidently, and purposefully. A relaxed sidewise stand is taken behind the cow. Care must be taken not to damage the tissues and organs of the rectum by poking or scraping.

The technician now lubricates the gloved hand and arm. Water is a sufficient lubricant; however, some prefer a mild lubricant such as K. Y. Jelly. K. Y. Jelly does not contain disinfectants which may irritate the cow's tissues and indirectly damage the sperm.

Once proper lubrication is completed the technician's steps are as
follows (1):

1. Gently rub the cow's anus with the wet fingers, inserting one
   and then several fingers held together, through the anal opening.
   With the fingers in a tight coned position the entire hand and
   as much of the arm as is needed can be passed into the rectal cavity.

2. Locate the cervix by gently pressing with the finger tips across
   the floor of the pelvis near the brim. The cervix may be ahead
   or behind the brim.

3. Pass the inseminating tube tip through the vagina and up the
   cervix.

4. Grip the cervix with the gloved hand and pass the inseminating
   tube tip into the cervical canal as far as it will go easily.

5. Manipulate the cervix so as to aid passage of the tube tip.
   Gently tilting up and down and moving forward and from side to
   side combining these movements into a circular motion is helpful.

6. May have to level the cervix with the tip of the tube. "Never
   jiggle the tube."

7. Hold the tip of the gloved forefinger at the forward limit of the
   cervix and when the tube reaches the finger----"ON TARGET." The
   semen is deposited. The tube should not enter the uterus as damage
   can easily occur.

8. "Never use force."

9. "Keep fingernails short."

Perry (18), on the other hand, disagrees with ABS on the point of semen

deposition. He states that for first service cows the inseminating tube
is usually passed through the cervix and just into the body of the uterus
where one-half to three-fourths of the semen is deposited. The tube is then
withdrawn to the mid-cervix where the remainder of the semen is left. For
repeat inseminations, it seems advisable to insert the tube to mid-cervix
only where all the semen is deposited so as not to interrupt a possible
pregnancy as some cows manifest heat after conception.

Additional investigation (4), however, goes on to dispute uterine
deposit of semen as mentioned by Perry. During natural service from the
male, the ejaculate is deposited in the anterior portion of the vagina on
or near the os or cervix. An exception is the horse as semen is ejaculated
through the cervix into the uterus because of the shortness of the cervix.

At the time of heat, when the female should be bred, there is an
increase in the secretion of mucus which becomes thin and flows through the
reproductive tract. Sperm naturally swim against currents and it is possible that the sperm cleanse themselves of bacteria as they fight against
the flow of mucus in the cervix on their way to the uterus.

Collections from the artificial vagina reveal the presence of bacteria,
some being the same species as those found in aborted fetuses. While freezing
may destroy many of these bacteria, swimming against a mucus-filled cavity
aids in removal of many remaining bacteria. Therefore, deposition of semen
into the entrance of the cervix more closely resembles natural breeding
than deposition within the uterus as practiced by many artificial insemination
cooperatives.

Research on this problem of deposition continues today.

Insemination after calving should occur at least sixty days after parturition so as to allow the reproductive tract to return to normal for better conception (23).

THE VALUE OF ARTIFICIAL INSEMINATION

Artificial insemination, as stated in the beginning paragraph, is at present extensively used with cattle, this use being based on a series of advantages to the technique.

1. The use of outstanding sires is increased (4), (23) as more than a hundred cows can be bred from semen of a single collection (3).

2. Bulls can be proven at a younger age (3), (4).

3. The farmer or rancher does not have to pay out the expense of keeping a sire (3), (23).

4. The possibility exists of mating outstanding animals although they are miles apart (23).

5. Valuable sires which because of injury, size, or other physical handicaps cannot make satisfactory natural service, may be used successfully with artificial insemination (23).

6. The percentage of conceptions is increased (4) as the possibilities of fertilization are increased when the female is inseminated a few hours before ovulation. Moreover, cows that habitually ovulate late could be inseminated after heat at which time she refuses to stand for the bull.

Following this same trend of thought, it is interesting to note that in natural copulation only a small proportion of the spermatozoa actually gain access to the uterus or ascend the tubes; the remaining portion being absorbed or extruded (3). But in artificial breeding a small quantity of semen can be placed with accuracy within the cervix; thus, a higher percentage

of the sperm gain access to the uterus. The result--a greater certainty
of impregnation and a considerable economy of sperm.

7. The danger of spreading genital diseases is greatly reduced (4),
(23). Herd infection of <u>Vibrio fetus</u> and <u>Trichomonas fetus</u>, both trans-
mitted by the bull and not easily detected in the cow, present difficult
problems in control (9). Introduction of a clean bull into an infected
herd will invariably result in his infection. Artificial insemination
will prevent this.

On the other hand, it may be desirable to introduce a trichomonad
or vibrio infected bull within an infected herd. The dilution factor alone
can greatly reduce the possibility of establishing infection in a clean
female, if artificial insemination instead of natural service is used.
Moreover, treatment of semen with antibiotics and glycerol and its preservation at low temperatures can greatly extend the usefulness of many infected but otherwise valuable sires.

8. Frozen semen permits a wider selection of bulls in a planned
breeding program (3).

9. In most cases better breeding and birth records are kept (23).

10. Artificial insemination permits the safe breeding of large bulls
to small heifers (3), (4).

The limitations of artificial insemination are not so much concerned
with the end result of the service, but with the actual methods of administration. The technique to be carried out successfully and safely requires
skilled persons in the fiàld (4), (23). It requires more time than natural
service (23) and also proper facilities for cleaning and sterilizing instru-
ments to be used. While the demand for superior bulls increases, the overall

demand for bulls decreases.

Artificial insemination success is most likely to follow adaptation of methods closely simulated to natural conditions (3). Knowledge of the natural processes of sperm production, natural insemination, and of fertilization is important in order to "meet" natural conditions. Deviation from the natural such that sperm cannot be maintained at body temperature when outside the body will not result in success.

CONCLUSION

Artificial insemination is not new but is an expanding technique. This paper has attempted to relate its history, its methods of administration, and its advantages and disadvantages. From all evidence, it appears that this technique is here to stay as it offers the modern livestock industry advantages both genetically and economically.

ACKNOWLEDGMENT

The writer wishes to express her sincere appreciation to the late
Dr. E. H. Herrick, Professor of Zoology, and Dr. A. L. Goodrich, Professor
of Zoology, for their assistance and professional advice in preparing this
report.

BIBLIOGRAPHY

(1) "American Breeder's Service Technicians Manual," Owner and Founder, J. Rockefeller Prentice, Chicago, 1960.

(2) Arey, Leslie Brainerd, PhD., Scd., LLD., Developmental Anatomy, W. B. Saunders Co., Philadelphia and London, 6th Edition, February, 1956.

(3) "Artificial Insemination of Dairy Cattle," Texas Agricultural Extension Service, G. A. Gibson, Director, College Station, Texas, L-58.

(4) "Artificial Insemination in Livestock Breeding," U. S. Department of Agriculture, Washington, D. C., Circular 567, October, 1940, revised April, 1962.

(5) Bonadonna, T., Le Basi Scientifiche e le Possibilita Techniche della Fecondazione Artificiale, Brescia, 1937 (Reference to Professor G. Amantea) in The Artificial Insemination of Farm Animals, Enos J. Perry, Rutgers University Press, New Brunswick, New Jersey, Third Revised Edition, April, 1960.

(6) "Bull Tales from KABSU," K. S. U. Department of Dairy Husbandry, Manhattan, Kansas, July, 1961, 12(5).

(7) Edwards, Joseph, "Male and Female Organs of Reproduction," in The Artificial Insemination of Farm Animals, Enos J. Perry, ed., 1960. Rutgers University Press, New Brunswick, New Jersey.

(8) Forgason, James, DVM., Winrock Farm Veterinarian, Morrilton, Arkansas. (Personal communication).

(9) Henderson, J. A., "Artificial Insemination," Diseases of Cattle American Veterinary Publications, Inc., 1956.

(10) Herman, H. A., PhD., and F. W. Madden, "The Artificial Insemination of Dairy Cattle," a Handbook and Laboratory Manual, Lucas Brothers, Columbia, Missouri, 1949.

(11) Herman, H. A., PhD., "Frozen Semen," in The Artificial Insemination of Farm Animals, Enos J. Perry, ed., Rutgers University Press, New Brunswick, New Jersey, 1960.

(12) Ivanoff, E. I., "On the Use of Artificial Insemination for Zootechnical Purposes in Russia," Journal of Agricultural Science, 12:244-256, 1922.

(13) Maximow, Alexander, and William Bloom, A Textbook of Histology, W. B. Saunders Co., Philadelphia, 1934.

(14) Oliver and Boyd, "The Technique of Artificial Insemination," Imperial Bureau of Animal Genetics, Edinburgh: 1933.

(15) Millar, P. G., and N. P. Ras, Manual of Infertility and Artificial Insemination in Cattle, Bailliere, Tindall and Cox, London, 1952.

(16) Perry, Enos J., John W. Bartlett, George Taylor, Joseph Edwards, Clair Terrill, Victor Berliner, and Fred P. Jeffery, The Artificial Insemination of Farm Animals, Rutgers University Press, New Brunswick, 1945.

(17) Perry, Enos J., John W. Bartlett, Joseph Edwards, Victor Berliner, Fred P. Jeffery, Ellis P. Leonard, J. A. Henderson, and Ralph P. Reece, The Artificial Insemination of Farm Animals, Second Revised Edition, Rutgers University Press, New Brunswick, New Jersey, 1952.

(18) Perry, Enos J., The Artificial Insemination of Farm Animals, Rutgers University Press, New Brunswick, New Jersey, Third Revised Edition, April, 1960.

(19) Prosser, J. J., B. S., E. J. Carroll, DVM., Leslie Ball, DVM., "Frozen Bull Semen—Collection Processing and Storage," Journal of the Society for Study of Breeding Soundness of Bulls, Colorado State Information Service, 8(2).

(20) Sisson, Septimus, S. B., B. S., The Anatomy of the Domestic Animals, W. B. Saunders Co., Philadelphia, Second Edition, 1914.

(21) Spallanzani, L., Tracts on the Natural History of Animals and Vegetables, Translated by J. G. Dalyell, Creech and Comstable, Edinburgh, Second Edition, 1803.

(22) Stamm, G. W., Artificial Breeding and Livestock Improvement, Edited by Dallas S. Burch, Windsor Press, Chicago, Illinois, 1954.

(23) Van Denmark, N. L., "Artificial Insemination," Revision of Better Farming Unit 55, Department of Dairy Science, College of Agriculture, University of Illinois, Urbana, Illinois, VAS 1002.

(24) Van Denmark, N. L., W. J. Miller, W. C. Kinney, Jr., Carlos Rodriquez, and M. E. Friedman, "Preservation of Bull Semen at Sub-Zero Temperatures," University of Illinois Agricultural Experiment Station, Urbana, Illinois, Bulletin 621, October, 1957.

(25) Walton, A., "The Technique of Artificial Insemination," Imperial Bureau of Animal Genetics, Edinburgh, 1933.

(26) Walton, A., and R. Prawochenski, "An Experiment in Eutelegenesis," Journal of Heredity, 27:341-344, 1956.

TECHNIQUES OF ARTIFICIAL INSEMINATION IN CATTLE

by

CAROLYN KEANE

B. S., Kansas State University, 1960

AN ABSTRACT OF A MASTER'S REPORT

submitted in partial fulfillment of the

requirements for the degree

MASTER OF SCIENCE

Department of Zoology

KANSAS STATE UNIVERSITY
Manhattan, Kansas

1963

The artificial insemination of livestock is not a new technique but one that dates back to the Arabs of the fourteenth century. Since that time it has come into wide use in many countries of the world. In 1954 the United States boasts that five million dairy cattle were in artificial insemination programs.

Artificial insemination is the deposit of collected semen into the cervical region of the female. This semen is collected by one of four methods: (a) vaginal collection; (b) massage; (c) use of electro-ejaculator; or (d) use of artificial vagina. The last method is the preferred as it is the quickest and easiest method whereby a complete physiological collection can be obtained.

After collection the semen is evaluated by a series of laboratory examinations: motility, methylene blue reduction test, sperm count, dead-alive count, and percentage of abnormalities. If the collection passes the necessary qualifications it is then diluted and placed in ampules for freezing.

The preferred extender is a yolk-sodium citrate-glycerol solution as it is not toxic to sperm, has an osmotic relationship similar to that of undiluted semen, has a pH favorable for continued viability, has a buffering effect which protects against marked changes in hydrogen ion concentration, does not cause a loss in fertility after long storage periods, and prevents injury due to cold shock.

The diluted semen is now bottled and prepared for freezing. The majority of artificial insemination laboratories freeze the semen in a bath of isopropyl alcohol or acetone and ground dry ice or liquid carbon dioxide. When minus 79°C. is reached, the ampules are transferred to storage tanks of dry ice or liquid nitrogen. Initial freezing in liquid nitrogen

vapor is a newly developed technique which may replace the alcohol-dry
ice bath provided the cost of liquid nitrogen lowers.

When needed an ampule is removed from the storage tanks and thawed
in an ice water bath. A technician draws the semen into a plastic inseminating tube. The cow is readied and by palpation the technician deposits
the semen in the canal of the cervix. Successful deposition should be
followed by conception and the birth of the calf.

As was expressed in the beginning paragraph, artificial insemination
is at present extensively used due to the following advantages:

1. The use of outstanding sires is increased.

2. Bulls can be proven at a younger age.

3. No expense of keeping sires.

4. The possible mating of outstanding animals.

5. Use of physically handicapped sires.

6. Percentage increase in conception rate.

7. Reduction of spreading genital diseases.

8. Frozen semen permits a wider selection of bulls in a planned
breeding program.

9. Better records are kept.

10. Safe breeding of large bulls to small heifers.
These advantages offer the livestock industry advancement both genetically
and economically.

CPSIA information can be obtained
at www.ICGtesting.com
Printed in the USA
BVHW040008160223
658552BV00005BA/135

9 781013 867231